Entrepreneurship

Entrepreneurship

Secrets to a Breakthrough

Ed K Chirara

To order additional copies of this book, contact:
Xlibris Corporation
0-800-644-6988
www.Xlibrispublishing.co.uk
Orders@Xlibrispublishing.co.uk
305467

Contents

Preface

My object of writing this book was to provide a brief and simplified summary of how one can sever his way through into entrepreneurship.

With the current global economic crunch, high job losses and less job creation, many face a bleak future. There is a few academic literature that teaches entrepreneurship, breaking it down to the reach of an ordinary person or mention the real furtive that lies in God's holy word, and readily accessible to the general reader. This manuscript is aimed at revealing some of those less-mentioned secrets that may transform your life. However, entrepreneurship is not meant to avert the economic crunch crisis, but to be a way of life and to help bringing you to financial freedom.

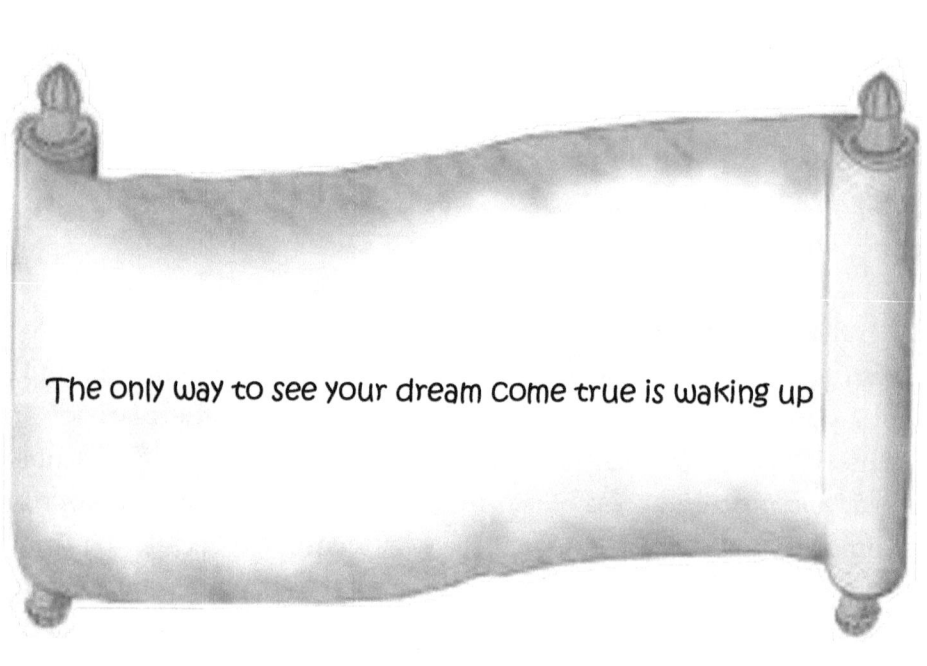

The only way to see your dream come true is waking up

Acknowledgements

I would like to take this opportunity to extend a special appreciation to my family for the initial support, allowing me the hours of research and typing. It wasn't easy. Many thanks to *Papa*, Professor E H Guti. You sowed this seed in me, now it has sprouted. To my mentor, the director of Forklift and Auto Services, Mr George Nyamuda, you were a real inspiration. My special thanks to my pastor, Macdonald Ndlovu, for nurturing me with the Word. I wouldn't have been who I am today.

I owe gratitude to my dad Mr J Chirara and the late Mrs S Chirara for their encouragement, care, and blessing. I am really proud of you. Mr Dave Ajayi of Ajayi Legal Chambers, words are not enough to express my gratitude. In your own special way, you made this manuscript a success. May God bless you richly.

E Chirara

Introduction

$\mathcal{J}$s being in business meant for a certain minority and not applicable to some? If not, why is it that some have tried it countless times, but to no avail? They experience failure, whereas others seem to succeed without any strand of struggle. Have you ever found yourself battling with similar questions, and still have no answers to them?

What could be the secret?

Not that we anticipate problems, but just for a moment, imagine yourself without your precious job, that breadwinner or whoever takes care of you. Do you see yourself able to survive another day, with bills, rentals, groceries, the list is endless. Well, that is where entrepreneurship comes in.

Being an entrepreneur does not necessarily mean making lots of money and becoming a millionaire overnight. It can simply be a source of extra income that takes you an extra mile, depending on the level you want to take it.

Africa has once been a victim of colonization. The colonial type of education was to train an employee and not an employer. You may agree with me that what our parents were encouraging us about whilst growing up, or even what most of us still convey to our children is that they study hard, pass so that at some point in life they get high-ranking, well-paying job.

Little do we encourage creativity. Whilst growing up, I have been observant on how our Asian counterparts conduct their lives. After school, instead of going home, kids do come to shops to assist. They are exposed to the business world at an early age, thereby developing an employer mentality in them. As they grow up, they do not see in themselves a potential employee, but an employer.

Whatever the cause might be, there is no more room to sit back, fold arms, and shift the blame on the past. It is time our community stands.

Now that you got hold of this handy book, can you take an expedition with me of the world our community is least informed.

Chapter 1

1. Entrepreneurship

*E*ntrepreneurship is a broad subject. In this manuscript, I will confine myself to economic entrepreneurship.

An entrepreneur is one who manages and organises a commercial undertaking.

If you take a closer look, you realise that there are three key words that make up this definition: manage, organise, and commercial.

*M*anage   *O*rganise   *C*ommercial

Manage

Managing can be defined as having something under one's control. For instance, one who has the post of a manager simply controls or directs the affairs or day-to-day running of a company or organisation.

Organise

To organise is to arrange in a systematic or orderly way in order to achieve a goal.

Commercial

A commercial is an undertaking done towards profit-making. It can be in the form of goods or services.

*B*usiness is more than just physical. It has a spiritual aspect as well. Taking a careful analysis and consideration of a couple of things, I have come to believe beyond any level of doubt that venturing into business is God's idea and unarguably a God principle. A principle is like a predetermined edict that one already knows the result.

God works with principles or laws that govern our daily living. Let's take a look at some of them.

A few examples are as follows:

> (a) The principle of *sowing*: . . . for *whatsoever a* man *soweth, that shall he also reap* (Gal. 6: 7, KJV), which is interpreted by our modern secular world as *the law of reproduction.*

> (b) The principle of *confession/imagination*: *A man shall be satisfied with the fruit of his mouth* (Prov. 18: 20–21), . . . *as a man thinketh in his heart so is he* (Prov. 23: 7, KJV), which is equally understood by the

world in quantum physics as *the law of attraction*. Law of attraction in Quantum physics says too much imagination or focus on a thing, either positively or negatively, the thing becomes real. Quite interesting, isn't it?

Do you think this could just be a coincidence that people pay out monies for charms and perform rituals for their businesses to proliferate? Of course not. It is simply because people are ignorant of God's word and His purpose for men.

There is also the principle of the *first fruits*. In the ancient times, when God gave new land to his people as a possession, they were supposed to take their first harvest of crops and bring it at God's place of worship. This was an act of worship and honouring God (Deut. 26: 1–2).

Honour the Lord with thy substance, and with the firstfruits of thine increase; . . . (Prov. 3: 9–10), which the African community interprets as one should bring his or her first salary to parents so that all may be well with him. All this becomes a counterfeit of God's original plan.

Now let us take a look at yet another fascinating principle. This one I prefer to call it the *works of hands* . . . . *that the Lord thy God may bless thee in the work of thine hand which thou doest* (Deut. 14: 29, KJV).

The Lord shall open unto thee his
good treasure, the heaven to give
the rain unto thy land in
his season, and to bless all
the work of thine hands.
(Deut. 28: 12, KJV)

In the *beginning*, when God created man, one of His initial plans for him, besides having dominion, was to take care of the garden and work it.

> *The Lord put man in the garden*
> *of Eden to care for*
> *it and work it.*
> (Gen. 2: 15, NCV)

Some seem to have mistaken this with a curse. When man sinned, God cursed the ground because of man, and He said, 'In toil shall man eat.' Simplified, meaning that man shall work harder than he would've had to. However, working had always been a God principle that invokes His blessing. *(Gen. 3: 17–19)*

It is God's desire to bless the work of men's hands, or rather entrepreneurial efforts.

If you go through the word of God, you realise that there is nobody who ever loved and obeyed God's word and lived a poor and miserable life.

Nevertheless, one has to take note of something here. You do the working with hands first, which is your duty, and then God will take care of the blessing. How about that?

2. Start-up

*V*enturing into business has its own challenges. I prefer to call this move a *leap of faith*. A person once said that the difference between doing business and gambling is that business is risking on a chance. That defines entrepreneurship. Our worst enemy is our mind. We always view things in the negative first as, *'What if it doesn't work.'* Little do we consider it in the positive as, *'What if it does.'*

Fear is like a dark room where negatives are produced.

3. My Dear Gift

There are three major keys to starting up a business. The first one is your *gift*:

> *A man's gift maketh room for him, and*
> *bringeth him before great men.*
> (Prov. 18: 16, KJV)

Your greatest tool in business is your area of strength. If you think of starting up a business, carefully identify your area of gifting.

If you consider great businesspersons in the world, including sportsmen, musicians, models, you name them, their secret is operating within their talent or gift. You simply ask yourself who you are, and what you are capable of doing, and then you invest in that.

4. Monkey See, Monkey Do Syndrome

The greatest mistake that has brought failure to many aspiring business people is the monkey see, monkey do practice.

In so many scenarios have we seen our friends and relatives doing things and seem to prosper, and then we conclude that our success lies on the same thing. To our surprise, we try it, only to realise that the end is nothing but failure.

Before investing, investigate

If you do what you know best, you can never go wrong. I strongly believe God has a great plan for every one of us.

> *For I know the plans I have*
> *for you, says the LORD.*
> *Plans of peace and not evil,*
> *to give you a future and hope.*
> (Jer. 29: 11)

Learn to identify yourself with the word of God personally. God looks at you as an individual.

A plan is a tactic or procedure laid out, which when one follows, will come out with the required result. Just like one constructing a structure, no matter how good the plan can be, if he refrains from following the drafted plan, he will likewise fail to produce quality work. Get to know God's plan over your life.

God is not a God of the present only. He is concerned about the future too. Now, the verse states that God has a plan for a peaceful future for you. Do not try to fix yourself into another person's plan. God has a specific plan for you.

5. Identify a Need

The other way of starting up a business can simply be, by identifying a need and coming up with a solution for a fee.

For example, you realise that the nearest groceries shop in your area is about three kilometres away from the residential area. This means that people have to walk quite a strenuous distance for them to get basic commodities.

You decide to open a small retail shop within your area and put a mark-up on your commodities; then you are in business. Needs are always there. You can hardly come across an area without them. We can't see them when we are not looking for them. Have you ever imagined how it feels, looking around and come up with something that somebody else failed to think about, or beat yourself up, when someone else does something that you keep asking yourself why you couldn't think of it?

6. Your Profession

You can use your profession as your key to business. What you are trained for is what you know best. More so if you are employed in that very field. Training gives you knowledge, and employment allows you to gain experience. For instance, a teacher can offer private lessons to students for a fee.

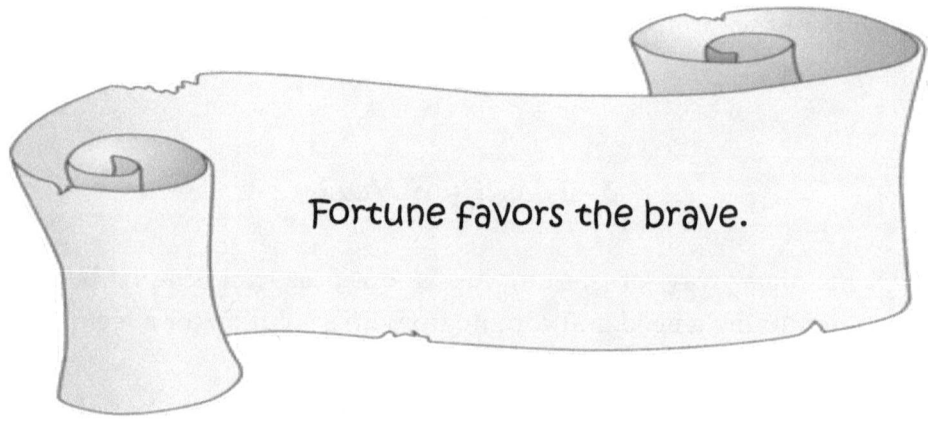

Fortune favors the brave.

Being in business does not necessarily mean starting up big. You do not despise humble beginnings *(Zech. 4: 10)*. At the mention of the word *business*, most people imagine a million-dollar empire. This becomes a hindrance, reducing or completely shattering their dreams of entrepreneurship. They believe that, for them to start up a business project, they need a $50,000 loan. The whole purpose of this manuscript is to provoke that entrepreneurial spirit in you, help you shift from a salary mentality, make you realise your potential, as well as giving you an idea on how to start.

Research

Know your game. Research on whatever you want to venture into, and gather as much knowledge as you can. You have to know your product source as well as your market target. Let's say you are into retailing. Suppliers of the product you want to trade in can be many on the market, having different prices. Learn to shop around and know the cheapest supplier. Every successful industry has its own secrets. Get to know yours.

What makes a good businessperson is being a good negotiator. Learn to push for a bargain. Do not just rush to buy. Some suppliers, with the knowledge that there are negotiators out there, they normally price their items with such an allowance. The art of negotiation starts with not accepting the first price of an item. Buying in bulk as well normally comes with discounts. It is wise to inquire with your supplier.

Be considerate. This doesn't mean you should engage in impulsive buying just for the sake of a haggle. Most products, especially perishables, do have expiry dates. You might regret, after suffering a loss of income and your profits, if your goods are not sold out within the stipulated period.

Market Research

There is no better way to starting up business than having an in-depth knowledge of your market. You cannot afford to do an experimental plunge into business. Of course, business may sound more-or-less like a risk, which can be true, but the good part is, it's a risk on a chance. You need to increase your chances of success. It's possible.

Feasibility study, better known as market analysis, is all you need as an entrepreneur. It gives you a clue on whether a market for your product or service exists. This survey also helps you.

- to know if there are any government regulations that restricts your nature of business. Each place has its own governing laws.
- with the data that gives you an idea on how much is needed financially to bring your business to its feet.
- to know the exact needs of your target market.
- to know your competitors. This can help you to device plans that can keep you afloat.

Some companies like Adidas were already players on the market, manufacturing sports gear, when Knight launched Nike Sportswear. Having realised an opportunity in an already dominated sportswear industry, Phil Knight founded Nike in 1964, offering more affordable products on the market.

Get to understand your area of business interest. Do what is known as *market research*. You can ask people within the area questions and get to know their needs. You can as well engage the use of questionnaires. Gather facts. This calls for one to think with his or her mind, and not the heart. Beware of letting your obsession to your business project cloud your judgment. You need to gather data based on the reality on the ground, making sure you leave no stone unturned.

Do not operate on assumptions. Your data will help you forge your way ahead.

Know your competitors. For instance, if there are dealers in your area doing the same business you are venturing into, see if you can afford to beat their prices, considering your source of supply. You do not just do business without considering competition. You might as well find yourself sitting in the cold. Have your back covered.

Keep your eyes open.

Opportunities

This is yet another way of starting up a business. An entrepreneur, according to the dictionary definition, is also known as an *opportunist.*

In life, if you do your survey, you realise that almost all things are seasonal. Commodities that may be in season in one area may not be in the other. Look for opportunities and use them. Have you ever realised that when a nation's economy collapses, resulting in the migration of people to other nations, others will be actually flocking in. Have you ever wondered why?

I observed something when the nation of Zimbabwe suffered a serious economic crunch, with hyperinflation reaching over a thousand percent. When many nationals flocked out in search for greener pastures, surprisingly, there was an influx of people moving into Zimbabwe, including some nationals who vowed not to go anywhere. The same happened with other nations like Zambia. What could be the secret?

Of course, these people see opportunities that others can't see. The Chinese and Nigerian communities are some of the few who learnt this secret. Many believe that they can only succeed in a place where the economy is flourishing.

Opportunity is missed by many people because it is often dressed in overalls (problems), and looks like work.
(T Edison)

Whilst others see a glass half empty, some see it half full.
(Author, Unknown)

William Colgate, founder of Colgate Palmolive, is one such man who kept seeing success and invested in a project his father had tried and failed and chose to resort back to farming, his former profession.

Your perspective matters.

The first step towards your breakthrough is thinking positively. Your second move is acting positively.

You can make it by utilising opportunities as they come by. At times, we become rigid and fail to think outside the box.

Chapter 2

Right People, Right Environment

*I*f you have chosen to soar like an eagle, then you have to stop hanging around with the chickens. 'Oops!', I know this is a tough one. A bitter pill it might seem to be, yet it brings healing to your body.

A man invests three things, namely *time*, *talent*, and *treasure*.

- ❖ Invest your *time* with men who inspire.
- ❖ Invest your *talent* with men who create.
- ❖ Invest your *treasure* with men who produce.

No man is an island. Get connected to people who went ahead of you in whatever business you want to venture into. Find a job in line with what you want to do if necessary, just for experience, even if it doesn't pay you too well. You must see beyond salary. Being in a job that is in line with what you want to do gives you an exposure. More and more knowledge is what you need. You need to have an idea of your product source and market. Know the challenges expected and how to tackle them.

It's always good to hang around people who are carrying the same vision with you, speaking the same language with you *(Luke. 1: 39–41)*. Mary hung around with Elizabeth, a person who carried an identical seed with her. It is not everyone who understands and believes in your dream.

> *Joseph dreamt a dream, and he*
> *told it to his brothers: and they hated*
> *him yet the more*
> (Gen. 37: 5, KJV)

Joseph's dream was good and true, but the problem came when he shared it with the wrong people. Wrong people are capable of giving wrong advice. Do not be ignorant of dream extinguishers out there. In life, at times, one has to make tough decisions. The people you spend more time with are the ones that determine your progress in life.

Who do you spend most of your precious time with? Is the person an inspiration to you in some area?

1. Acquire Knowledge

Gather as much literature (books) as possible, pertinent to what you want to do. Visit the Internet and do some research. Attend business seminars. Knowledge is a long-term investment.

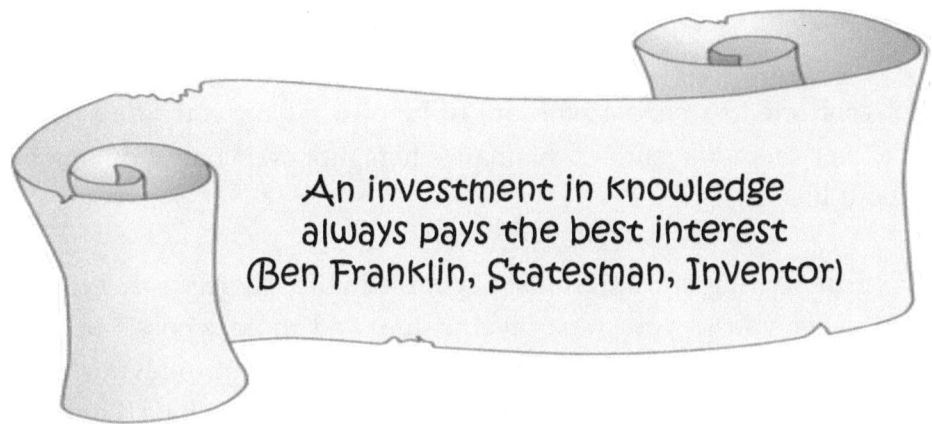

An investment in knowledge
always pays the best interest
(Ben Franklin, Statesman, Inventor)

It is never too late to learn. The man George Dawson was a son to a black slave in the ancient America. He never got an opportunity to go to school. Meaning he was illiterate until the age of ninety-eight, when he made up his mind to start learning. To many, it is an age of no hope. By then, he did not know even the alphabet. Two years later, he could read his birthday cards on his own. Before he passed away at the age of 103, he had written a book titled *Life is so good*. A school was built and named in honour of him. Right now, he is an inspiration to many. Never tell yourself that you are too old to learn, neither should you tell yourself that you are still too young, so you still have all the time in the world.

Invest in knowledge. Thank God, there are even a lot of online schools nowadays. This allows you to study at your own time in line with what you are venturing into.

Knowledge is power. There is an idiom in the shona language, which says, *An ignorant man is just as good as a dead man.*

2. Connections

Get connected to people who are of help in taking you to a higher level. Let's face the truth of the matter here; not everyone is of benefit to your life.

There are two significant groups of people in life. There are those who help usher you to your next level in life, and those whose purpose is simply to take you down. Not all people are meant to favour you. Hear me and hear me good, this has nothing to do with hate. Love all, but always know whom to consort with. Gather wisdom, and do not despise it.

> *For by wise counsel thou shalt*
> *make thy war; And in multitude of*
> *counsellors, there is safety*
> (Prov. 24: 6, KJV)

Stay surrounded by people who inspire you. It is time you bring some people in your life, and as well cut off some.

You must be willing to face criticism, if you really want to get somewhere in life. If you happen to meet someone who is bold enough to point out your weakness, you would better stick to such a person, for he is more than just a friend. Being human, we love hearing things that make us feel good only, even when it doesn't build us.

Anything of significance that you achieve under the sun has a price to pay. It doesn't just come on a silver platter.

What Do You Have in Your Hand

*E*ach time when God wanted to do something of significance through a person, he would ask what one has. It did not have to be big, but it was more like a *point of contact*.

All that Moses had in his possession was a rod, and this simple rod did God use to do mighty exploits *(Exod. 4: 2–3)*. The same applies to the widow of Zarephath, *(1 Kgs. 17: 10–12)*, the widowed prophet's wife, *(2 Kgs. 4: 1–5)*, and the list is endless. At times, nature makes us believe that we need more to make more.

Real wealth and financial breakthrough have been without doubt associated with people who chose at one moment in life to take a leap of faith into business than resorting to seeking a job. Though there is nothing wrong with being employed, but employment, one once said pays you enough to report for work the following morning. I am yet to meet a millionaire employee.

I can support this with a scriptural list of successful men and none of them ever became successful by serving for the rest of his life. However, you do not necessarily have to quit your job to be an entrepreneur, if you are employed, unless you feel it's necessary to do so.

Jacob served Laban for a couple of years *(Gen. 29)*, but a time came when he had to move with his family and wealth.

Isaac sowed in that land, and received
in the same year hundredfold: and the
LORD blessed him . . . He waxed great

and went forward, and grew until he
became very great.
(Gen. 26: 12–13, KJV)

As I mentioned earlier on, being an entrepreneur does not necessarily mean quitting your job suddenly. It could simply be a supplement to your income. Most people suffer from the salary syndrome. Know that you can do better, if only you start thinking outside the box. Think beyond your salary.

Business is like sowing with expectance of a harvest one day. If you fear sowing, the seed might as well be rendered useless in your hand. In this current economic world, we are talking of inflation.

Great risks, great profits.

A step into business is a step of faith. Imagine a farmer burying seeds in the ground. If his worst fear is his seeds failing to germinate, do you think he would ever sow?

Life is like a deep pool, either you swim or you sink.

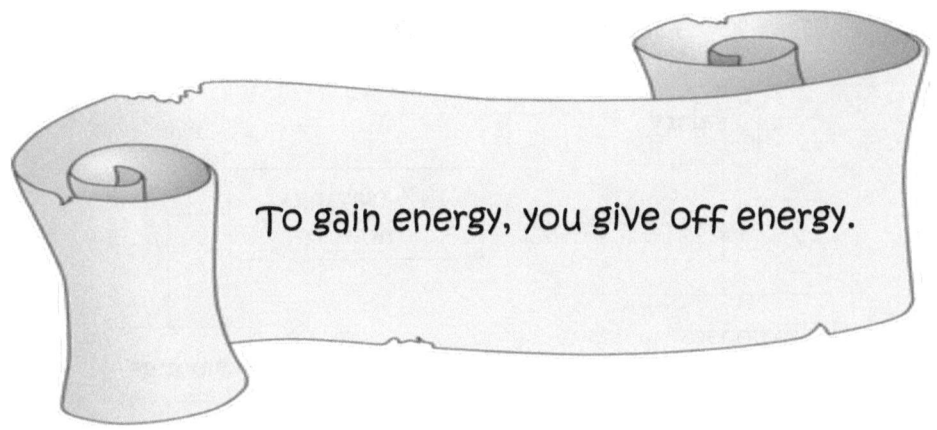

To gain energy, you give off energy.

In chapter 3, under the head *Financing*, we are going to talk about different ways of financing your start-up business. Chapter 7 has information on saving.

Here is a simplified illustration that can be of help in saving for a start-up business. From as little as 10 per cent of your total income accumulated over a couple of months or years can serve as capital to start up your business without borrowing. This can be used as well when you are generally saving up.

Save, for saving saves.

Personal Financing Plan (PFP)

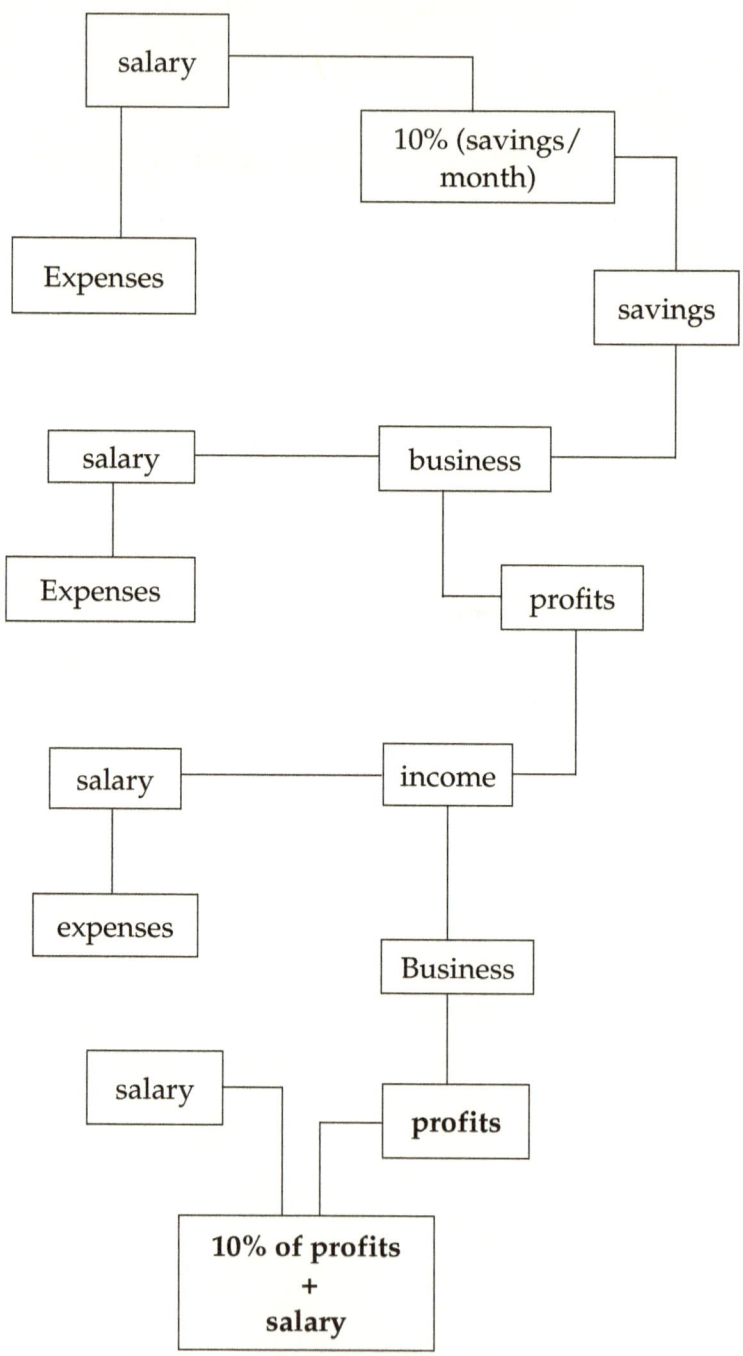

Dream On

*D*ream, dream, dream on. Your future lies in your dreams. Absolutely nothing in life is by chance. What you see is what you get. You need to have a vision and purpose for your business. What you see yourself as in your dreams gives birth to your future. From the foundation of the earth, every existing thing your eyes can see was once just a plan in one's mind. God saw man before He created him. He described His intended creation to other heavenly hosts.

> *And GOD said, let us make man in our own*
> *image, after our likeness:*
> (Gen. 1: 26, KJV)

Learn to put things in ink and paper. Many people find it easier to own diaries that they jot down their past, both the good and the bad, than writing down their future plans. Write your dreams down. A human is not a supercomputer. We tend to forget as time goes by. Something written down, you can at least revisit it. One once said the faintest ink is better than the finest memory.

Research shows that an average person only utilises an average of about 3.5 per cent of their brain (thinking capacity) in their lifetime. Most of the geniuses would have utilised about 5 per cent. In African circles, a myth goes like, *'too much of thinking or studying can cause one to go crazy.'* Well, this is yet to be proven. Don't you think we would have been having lots of crazy people in nations leading in technology? Most people are lazy to think. Don't be one of them. You need to have your quiet moments, whereby you do nothing else but think and come up with creative ideas. Most of the time we seem to be content with other people's creations, and as well wait impatiently for their next inventions. Refuse to be ordinary. Be innovative.

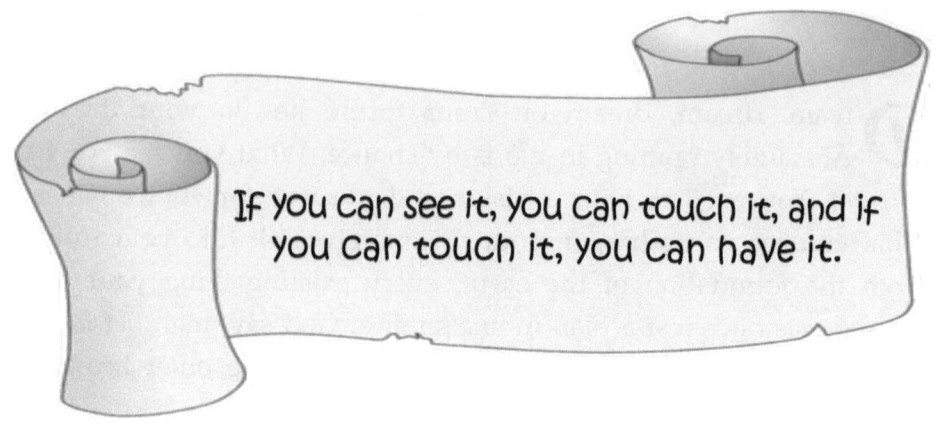

If you can see it, you can touch it, and if you can touch it, you can have it.

For a dream cometh through
the multitude of words . . .
(Eccles. 5: 3, KJV)

Redeem the Time

*P*rocrastination is a thief of time. There is no better time than 'now'. Business opportunities are seasonal. When an opportunity arises, seize it because it does not last forever.

Boast not thyself of tomorrow;
for thou knowest not what a day brings forth.
(Prov. 27: 1, KJV)

The power to control your tomorrow lies in your hands today. Whatever your hands find to do, do it hastily. Procrastination at times feels good. It feels as if you have all the time in the world. The thing that we never think of is that God provided a twenty-four-hour day for everyone of us. No one has more, and likewise, no one has less.

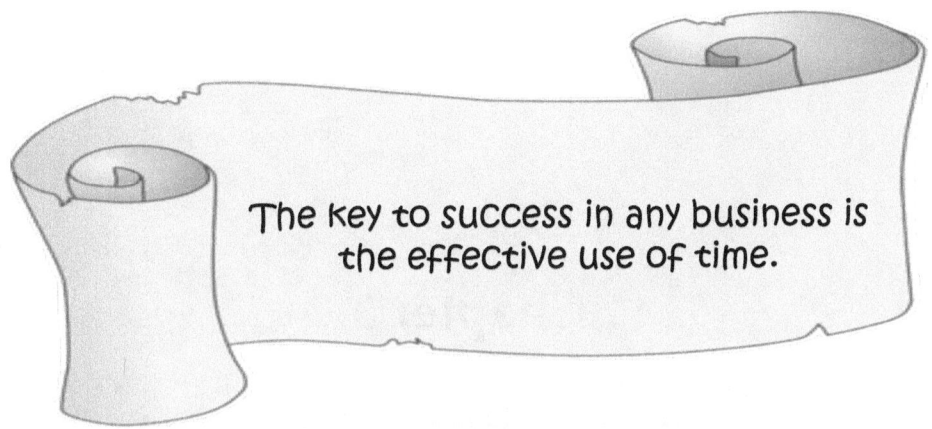

The key to success in any business is the effective use of time.

Always fight with your eyes open. Make use of a planner. Each day of your life, you should be knowing what you are going to do and the time you are going to do it. Don't just live in confusion. Even ants know seasons and prepare. You don't expect to see ants and termites hassling for food in the peak of winter.

Never close your eyes on the reality in front of you. Keep adapting to changing times. Do not ignore signs of change around you. If you realise a shift in your business, be ready for improvement or rather diversification.

Chapter 3

Launching Your Business

1. Things to Consider

Chapters 1 and 2 are intended to prepare your mind and make you realise your infinite potentials. Now that you have a handle on what it is that is expected of you, it's time to put your desire into action.

First, with the help of these previous chapters, identify what you want to trade in. Sit down, plan, and write down your business concept. This should be able to make one see your vision as it is in your mind. It can be of help as well if you are expecting a funding.

> *Write the vision and make it plain*
> *upon the tablets, so that he that*
> *readeth may run with it.*
> (Hab. 2: 2, KJV)

Your proposal should convincingly give a reason for one to buy your idea. Be as candid as possible.

Here is an outline of what we call the *what, where, why, how* concept. These are the easiest steps one can use as a guide when drafting a business plan.

Your project plan should at least carry the following:

- *Vision Statement:* It is a concise outline of the purpose and goals of your business. This carries your *Problem Statement* that shows the need that you realised.

- *Business Profile:* Define and describe your intended business and the procedures. Try to stay focused on the specialised market you intend to serve. State your *Project Justifications,* which indicates the need for your solution or service. Remember the example of a need to supply basic commodities in chapter 2 *(Identify a Need).*

- *Proposed Approach:* This indicates to detail how you are planning to tackle the problem. Whilst compiling this, avoid trying to be one you are not. Indicate to detail where there may be a need to hire. We have different areas of strength.

- *SWOT Analysis*: On this, you have to be true to yourself. This is where you identify and state your Strengths, Weaknesses, Opportunities, and Threats. This is based on your research. Gather and exhaust all data required.

- *Projected Budget*: Here, you are looking at how much you would need for your business project to commence smoothly until it starts generating income. Of course, you need that allowance since you will still be setting your feet on the ground. Clients or customers will still be getting to know you on the market.

Before you start your business, no matter how small or big, first check whether you have enough *capital* to launch and sustain it.

*For which of you intending to
build a tower, sitteth not down
and counteth the cost whether
he has enough to finish it.*
(Luke 14: 31, KJV)

Start by doing a breakdown of all costs expected, based on the data you would have amassed. You may need the help of a person with an accounting knowledge to help you compile your data.

2. Financing

Now let us look at your business' *financing*. Some business projects need more finances than others, some less, and some none at all. Especially when you are offering services, your input may perhaps be your know-how and strength. If you are into production, you would need raw materials, transport, and probably workforce. Bear in mind that there might be need for you to sustain your business before it can sustain itself and you. Depending on your means of financing, you can implement the PFP idea stated in the illustration in chapter two's *What Do You Have In Your Hand*.

There are so many ways you can have your project financed.

- You can personally finance your project from your savings. This is my most preferred way of financing. You do not have to stress about interests, or fear having to lose your valuables in case you fail to pay back as agreed. It just doesn't feel good knowing that you owe. You can start saving towards your project.

- You can sell your idea to a good friend or relative, who is financially buoyant to finance your project. Agree on when you think you can afford to pay back. The advantage on this one is the financier might be willing to help and not demanding an interest. However, this is not a passport to abuse such privilege. You have to honour your agreement. At times we tend to take for granted those people close to us, knowing that they might not have the guts to take harsh actions towards us.

- You can use the bank or other financing institutions. However, the disadvantage can be their requirements. They might require collateral security. They reserve the right to approve or disapprove your proposal.

- Though there are a few challenges on this one, some do employ the *partnership strategy*. There are two major forms of capital namely, money and assets and services.

  You may not have capital, for instance, in monetary form, yet you have the know-how or assets that you can plough into the business. All you need to do is look for a reliable and trustworthy entity offering any one of the forms of capital that you don't have to partner with you. Partnership may involve a lot of other conditions that may seem unfavourable, like limited power on decision-making as well as agreements on share-stakes, as compared to being a sole-proprietor. You may feel like your freedom to run things the way you want is restricted, which may affect your enthusiasm. Another thing you should expect in a partnership as in sole-proprietorship is unlimited liabilities. This means that you are responsible for the company's debts, meaning that your personal assets are bound to be attached to your business in case your company owes and it can't afford to settle its debts. In the case of a partnership, you are equally responsible for your partner's debt in business. Everything has its own advantages and disadvantages.

Things may seem slow, but taking you somewhere.

Never take things for granted. Arguments are bound to rise in partnership, be it you are friends or even close relatives. There is always a need for a written agreement. It's wiser to draft an agreement that will govern your operations. Never rely on verbal agreements.

3. Priorities

L earn to put first things first. Never postpone what is meant to be done today to tomorrow. Always give priority to the right thing, no matter how small it might seem to be. The worst thing you can ever do is to be busy, but not effective. Avoid directing your energy to wrong areas.

Eliminate anything that does not work towards the establishment or enhancing the progress of your business. Always see to the end whatever you would have started. Never leave things half done.

Customer Care

R esearching is one of your major tools to success when running a business. Never be content with the service you offer.

1. The Blue Ocean Strategy

If you are trading in goods, always fight to improve the quality of your product than putting your focus onto your competitors. There are so many competitors on the market selling products similar to yours. One question you need to ask yourself is, 'What should make one leave the rest and consider my product or services?' If you have an answer to that, then you are on the right track. Move with the times. Know what the living generation wants. Believe me; what made our grandpas and grannies' jaws drop, may not move us in the now generation.

It reminds me of those days, when afro-hair and perm were the vogue, and when almost every young person was so crazy about country music. Generations have come and gone. If you are to mention that to the current generation, they would not even understand what you are talking about. Now, we do not need typewriters anymore. We are now living in the world of computers. Keep *au fait* with changes.

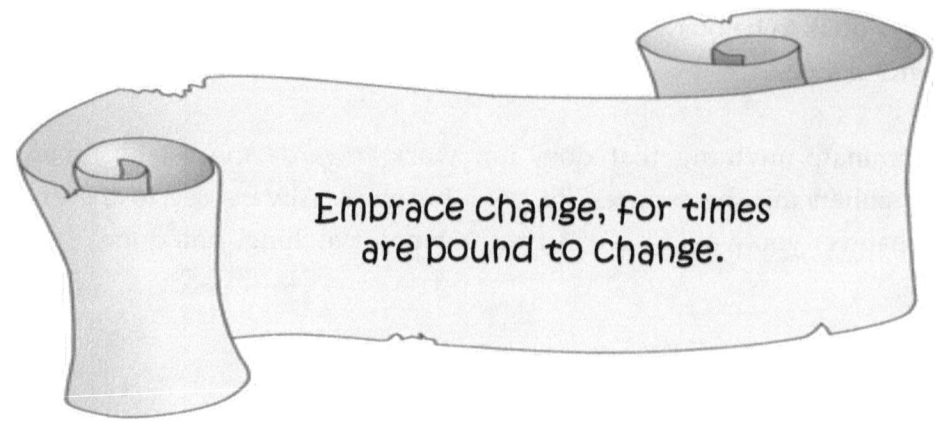

Embrace change, for times
are bound to change.

2. Services

If your business offers services, then you have to look at the quality of your services. Are you reliable and efficient? Do you maintain a personal touch with your clients? Never take a client for granted just because you know them. Many people lose business opportunities due to lack of professionalism. They think that because they know you, so you can understand and be the least to be served, or have your job shoddily done.

Never promise what you cannot deliver. Sounding professional is different from being professional. If you lack professionalism, in no time, you would lose your clients faster than you got them.

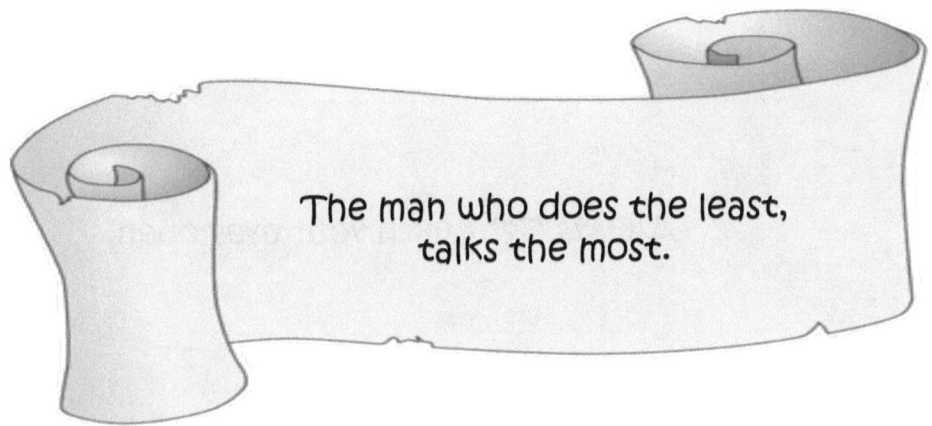

The man who does the least,
talks the most.

Measure your breakthrough by your clientele base, not by the profits you have made. Why do I say this? Well, clients may come to you in a moment in time probably before they notice your exorbitant prices and lose confidence in you. Once they do, you realise them not coming back to you. This will then give you large profits one morning, and the next morning nothing. Especially when your business is still at its infancy, put as much focus as you can to building a clientele base than making money. You will realise that money will follow.

Correct Costing

*a*lways watch out for your pricing. This falls in two parts. *Undercharging* leads to a loss. You may have all the clients in the world, and later on be grounded. The whole idea behind entrepreneurship is making profits.

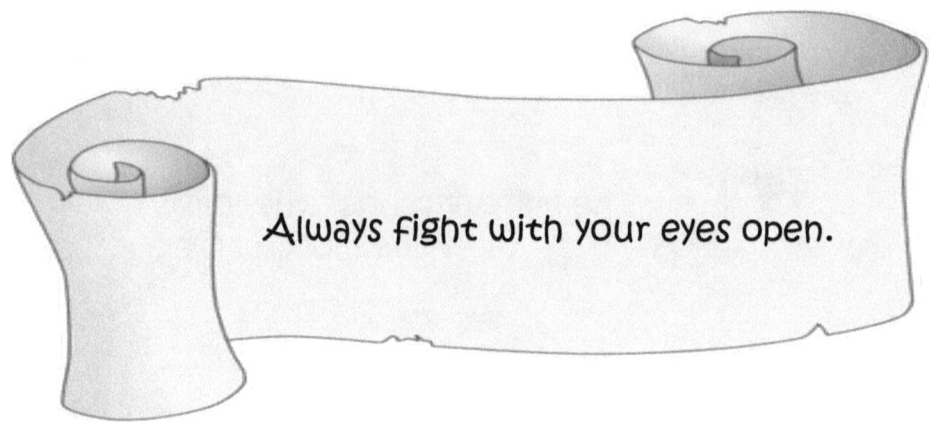

Always fight with your eyes open.

Overcharging can cost you clients. You might find yourself with many customers for a while, but later on, you will be out of business. Always stay aware of fluctuating prices around you. Remember, you are in a battlefield. For you to get your market share, you need to be vigilant.

There are two ways to make money—increase sales and decrease costs. (Steve Kaplan, Author)

Marketing

*N*ot having clients does not necessarily mean you are trading in the wrong line of business. It could be, because people do not know about you. That is where marketing comes in.

A woman born to a family of Hungarian immigrants to the United States, by the name Josephine Esther Mentzer (Estee Lauder), worked with her uncle who was a chemist or skin specialist, where she may have got some inspiration. Later on, she launched her own cosmetics business, in which she started by doing intensive door-to-door demonstrations of her products. With time, she secured a corner space in a departmental shop and next, in various leading retail shops. That is how Estee Lauder cosmetics company was birthed.

Estee Lauder has become a household name in the cosmetics industry. The secret was rigorous marketing.

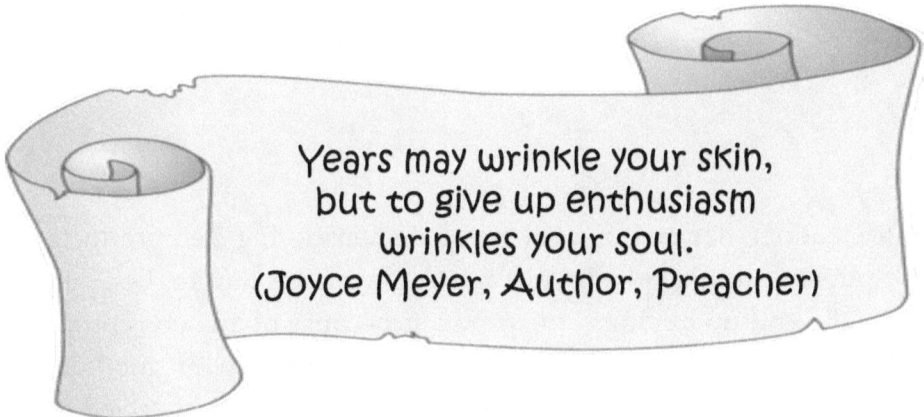

Years may wrinkle your skin,
but to give up enthusiasm
wrinkles your soul.
(Joyce Meyer, Author, Preacher)

Shout out loud. Do not be silent. Tell the world about yourself. If success is to be on the list of your achievements, you would better have marketing as one of your top priorities. Seek professional marketing knowledge. Poor marketing skills and techniques can cost you dearly.

Marketing is like waving a hand in one's face for attention. We need that attention. If you are in a situation where people can't come to you, then it means you need to go to them.

Spend on advertising, for it pays off. There are so many ways used in advertising. Here are some of them. You can employ the use of the press, posters, radio, even street or door-to-door campaigns. Get to know the laws that govern your area first. Some would require you to have a license to do so. Some business people even bring in the idea of promotions (competitions), offering an attractive prize. You have to do whatever it takes to draw the attention of clients or customers to your products.

Big companies do not advertise because they are big. They are big because they advertised.
(Author, Unknown)

Estee Lauder devised a strategy of demonstrating her products to the public, and it worked. With major players on the market, people normally end up buying some products because of a good reputation that would have existed for a long time. That's why goodwill is considered part of the company assets. People are attracted to a person or product they can trust. They as well consider affordability. If it worked for her, it may work for you.

Chapter 4

Be Professional

Your Business and You

*Y*our business is a *legal entity*. Treat it like an individual who has rights. By the way, misuse of your company's funds is a federal crime. Do proper filing and accounting of business funds. Be an employee to your business and put yourself on a salary. A more successful month does not mean a higher salary than usual. It sounds harsh, isn't it? However, that is the secret to the top.

1. Be Consistent

Clients are quite observant. They are watchful of how you operate more than you think. Stick to your operating hours. You would rather extend your working hours than opening late or closing earlier than your indicated times.

Those things you may consider petty can be offending to clients. When you are in business, clients are the life blood to your business.

So, trustworthiness is one thing you can't trade for anything. Always make sure you give a prompt attention to clients' needs and concerns.

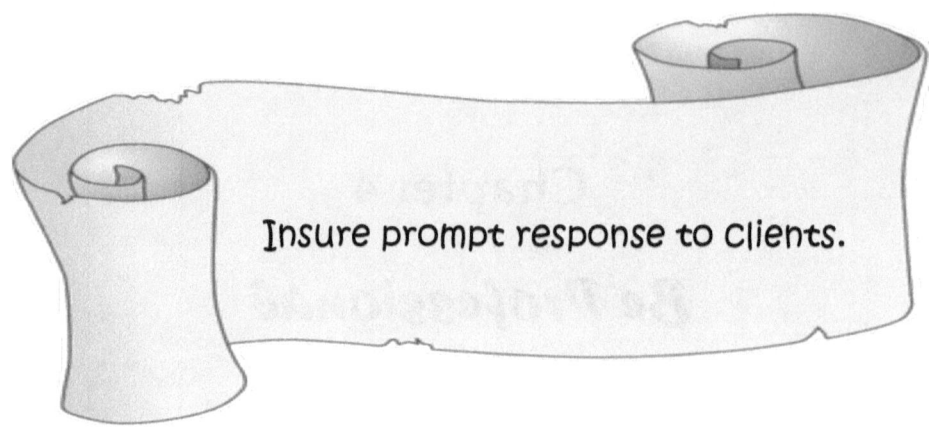

Insure prompt response to clients.

Never hoodwink a client. Do not promise the moon and stars. It's better to under-promise and over-deliver than to raise higher expectations. Always mention what you can deliver. Faithfulness matters, no matter how hard it might be. There are two crucial things one has to labour for, and that is respect and trust. Respect is earned, and trust is gained. Always remember that trust is easily lost than gained. So, never trade it for anything. Always deliver in time.

An apology does you no harm, but actually pays off. Learn to apologise, and give immediate attention to the problem.

2. Be Captivating

Have you ever asked yourself why big brands change the look of their products now and then? Ooh yes! Your product should always be alluring. The market is like one pool, with many fishing rods cast into it. Now the question is, how catchy is your bait? New, young, and innovative players keep on coming on the same market. If you do not stay vigilant, you can find yourself drowned in the ever-rising pool of competition and never be remembered again. Always keep up a high standard of goods and services. Insure quality, eye-catching packaging, if you are into production or repackaging. This includes your choice of colours. Know the colours that go with your product. For instance, there are colours that go with the food industry, babies' products, men's products, women's, etc. Your choice of a brand name matters too. The name has to make a statement in one's mind.

A maintained personal touch with clients wins you their hearts. This is a psychological game. Try as hard as possible to know your clients by name. There is nothing so sweet to a person than to hear the mention of his name. Greet them by name, and keep them posted on your product offers. If there is anything that makes a human to feel good is when he feels appreciated. Just a thank you does you no harm. These seemingly miniature things can catapult you to your breakthrough. So do it right the first time. Just knowing that someone out there cares for you gives one a reason to perpetually want to turn back to you. Smartness is a charm. Nobody likes to be associated with uncleanness, even the dirtiest person on earth. Everyone wants to be allied with good things. Untidiness speaks of laziness.

Diligence

In life, there is absolutely no room for laziness. In fact, God hates laziness. There are times we judge situations with a human perspective, and then standoff and conclude that there is no solution, instead of acting.

Laziness would rather consider the amount of effort needed to have work done than the amount of work covered. You should do whatever it is that needs to be done, despite what it takes.

The writer says thus:

> *The sluggard will not Plough*
> *by reason of the cold; therefore*
> *shall he beg in harvest,*
> *and have nothing.*
> (Prov. 20: 4, KJV)

The book of Genesis says Isaac sowed in a season of famine, and the result was a hundredfold harvest. Be willing to work. Remember what I mentioned in chapter 1. Just fulfil your duty of working with your hands, and leave to GOD the blessing duty.

At one moment, the writer directed a lazy person to an anthill. He urges him to go and see how ants, small as they are, work without a king (supervision), and how they know seasons. Laziness judges work to be done by the amount of effort required instead of achievements.

You have to conquer your fears. Mostly, people tend to fear the unknown. Stop giving unnecessary excuses.

> *The slothful man saith, there is a lion*
> *in the way; a lion in the streets.*
> (Prov. 26: 13, KJV)

Staying in your cocoon can never change anything. In fact, things get even worse. It's better you risk on a chance than never. At times you need to make radical choices in life.

> *They said to each other, 'why*
> *Do we seat here until we die?*
> *There is no food in the city. So*
> *If We go into the city we will*

die there. If we stay here we
will die. So let's go to the
Aramean camp. If they let
us live, we will live. If they kill
us we will die.'
(2 Kgs. 7: 3–4, NCV)

There were three all-risk choices for the four lepers here, yet they had to choose one. They chose the one that had higher chances. Although it sounded risk going to the Arameans, that's where there was hope for food.

Hard work is needed to confront issues, weaknesses, and inconsistencies.

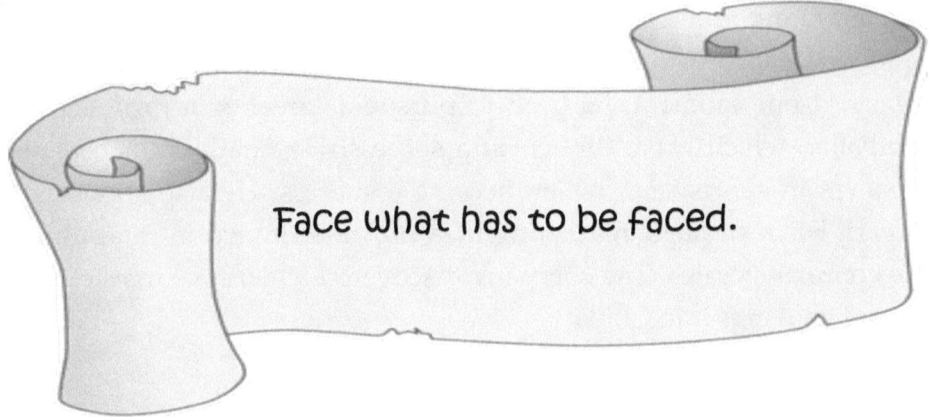

Face what has to be faced.

Focus

You may have too many ideas, and still have more coming, but you need to focus. Just like a golfer who focuses on one ball at a time, aiming one hole and with one target, being the winner.

I therefore so run, not as
uncertainly; so fight I, not

as one that beateth the air.
(1 Cor. 9: 26, KJV)

Just like on a car, although the headlamps may be lighting up, still you need to frequently take it for light-focusing. Light is good, but if directed at the wrong place, then the whole point is lost.

Rather stick to one idea and develop it than trying to chase many at a time. Don't be a jack of all trades, for you will definitely be a master of none. No matter how long the route you take to reach your destination may seem to be, never lose focus along the way.

A lesson is learnt from a man of German descent by the name Herbert Hainer, founder of Adidas Sportswear. Hainer started by working in a family butchery, before he moved on to start his first business project, a bar. At one moment, he tried to pursue a career as a professional footballer, which wasn't much of a success. He finally launched his business in sportswear, which became a success. He also sponsored Bayern FC, a strategic marketing idea that contributed in catapulting the company's sales. The company discovered a lucrative market and spread its wings into China.

Integrity

If there are two most difficult words to say in life, that will be *'sorry'* and *'no'*. However, they are the same words that can either make you or break you.

Author Roger Fritz mentioned in his book, *Building Your Legacy*, that 'In listing your assets, start with things money can't buy. For example-Integrity'.

A good name is better than
precious ointment,
(Eccles. 7: 1, KJV)

An apology brings healing, but a *no* keeps you from falling into unnecessary regrets. Sometimes a 'no' brings about a sense of guiltiness in us. Naturally as human beings, we have a soft spot in us. We tend to accept what our innermost being is not ready to accept, just because we want to impress.

Guard your dignity with your life, for it is easily lost than gained. Value it like an asset. Crazy as this may sound, your dignity relies more on your No's than Yes'.

The same applies also in negotiating. Some things, despite how much you want them, don't always be the cheap one. A 'let me think about it' does the magic. It leaves the other part anxious. That's how the art of negotiation works.

Negotiation is like a game—the one to break first is the loser.

Chapter 5

Don't Give Up the Fight

S ometimes because of the tough situations we go through, another part of us whispers to us to quit. When you are going through hell, do not stop.

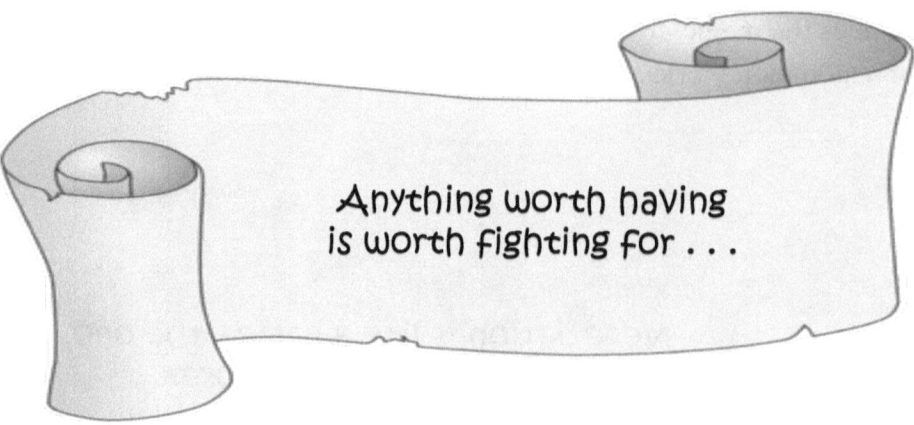

Anything worth having
is worth fighting for . . .

Fight effectively for the well-being of your business. Do an analysis. Identify issues that may be hindering you from reaching your goals and bringing the best out of your business. Seek advice from relevant people.

Winners are fighters who do not quit. Direct your energy strategically, and focus on maximizing your business. Avoid listening to people of negative speech. Victory starts in the mind before the real act in the physical. Always think positively.

When others saw goliath a giant too big to fight, David was seeing a giant too big to miss.

Persistence pays off. Strive Masiyiwa, founder of Econet Wireless, is one African brother who inspires me a lot.

Born in the early sixties in Zimbabwe, Strive rose to become one of Africa's richest, after tirelessly fighting in prayer and in courts for five years, just to obtain a telecommunications license to enable him to launch his much wanted cellular network company. By then, the rights were solely owned by the state, making it impossible for anyone to venture into a business of that nature. Some offered him an easy way out by asking for a bribe; he, knowing his stand as a born-again Christian and child of God, declined such an offer, and God saw him through. Through much resistance saw the birth of Econet Holdings. A short while, he had launched Mascom in neighbouring Botswana and Econet in several African nations, reaching to as far as Nigeria.

He broke record by becoming the youngest recipient of the Businessman of the Year Award in Zimbabwe. He also received various awards and has become a role model to many upcoming entrepreneurs. To date, he has covered over fifteen countries in Africa, Europe, USA, Latin-America, and in the Asia-Pacific. The way you perceive situations matters.

As a man thinketh in his heart, so is he . . .
(Prov. 23: 7, KJV)

Success lies in the mind. You have to win the battle in the mind first.

Whilst others saw grasshoppers in themselves, Caleb and Joshua, despite seeing the giant descendants of Anak, saw conquerors in themselves too. In fact, grasshoppers do not eat grapes. Grasshoppers are wanderers. They do not have a decent habitation. In other words, the other group had disqualified themselves from God's promise in the spirit realm. Who do you see in yourself? See a vanquisher in yourself, and you will become one.

Aim to be a world changer. You have to leave a mark of your existence on earth. To me, success is not determined by how much you made in your lifetime, but by having fulfilled your purpose on earth. I have come to observe that the Bible comprises of two major characters. The people who are mentioned by name, mostly were either the best or the worst. The rest were included amongst the crowds. This shows us that there is no room for mediocrity *(Rev. 3: 16)*. Either you are in or you are out.

If you tried once, try twice. If you tried twice, do it again. Keep fighting! Keep up the good fight, and never give up.

Don't Live with Death

a void dwelling in the past losses. Sometimes, because of our past experiences, we have a propensity of having our future determined by our past. Each time we try to do the right thing, we feel like that past misfortune is going to pay us yet another visit.

Do not live with death; bury it. You might have tried something and failed, simply because you did not apply the right strategies.

You can only correct what you are willing to confront

Always think with your mind, not with your emotions. Take your time to make a decision. You would rather consult than decide when emotional, because decisions birthed out of emotions are often wrong. Nobody has power to change his or her past, but all of us have control over our destiny. It's not how you started that matters, but how you end it. It is also interesting that almost every person God used in the ancient times has a wobbly, messy past to point at as an excuse. Abraham came from a family that was into idolatry, Moses murdered a man, Gideon was the least, born from the weakest family, Jephthah was son to a harlot, David was born out of wedlock, Solomon was born to Bathsheba. Jabez was born in pain, and he was named pain. If they would have given in to the pressures of their past, they wouldn't have made history that we are reading about this day. You might be a victim of an ugly past, but this shouldn't determine your future.

You might have at some point in life tried some business and you failed. Do not beat yourself up. Rather turn it into a lesson.

Use what you have been through as wind beneath your wings.

Losers are winners who quit. You may have failed the first time, but what does God say about you?

Scripture says,

> remember ye not the former
> things, neither consider the
> things of old. Behold I'll
> do a new thing;
> (Isa. 43: 18, KJV)

Theologians say the statement *'fear not'* appears about 365 times in the Bible. This goes without saying, there is a 'fear not' for you every single day of your life. Cast away your fears, and do it again.

Faith comes by hearing, hearing the word.

> Peter said, 'Lord, if it
> is really you, then command

me to come to you on the water.
Jesus said, 'come.'
(Matt. 14: 28–29, NCV)

Peter understood something here, that others couldn't. All he needed was a word from the Lord to activate this seemingly impossible thing. It doesn't matter what you went through, if God says, *'yes'*, then do it again.

Experience Not Experiment

Gaining experience seems to be the best thing to do. It is gained in the field and not on the desk. If you are working and not ready to quit your job for a full-time service in your business, you may engage a reliable person to run it for you, but, whatever it takes, it is advisable to be hands-on on your project. Spare time when you knock off, to monitor operations. Be well vest with how things run, not by word of mouth. There are certain angles of your business that you can never understand and serve well unless you are involved in its day-to-day operations. You make mistakes, and you learn from them.

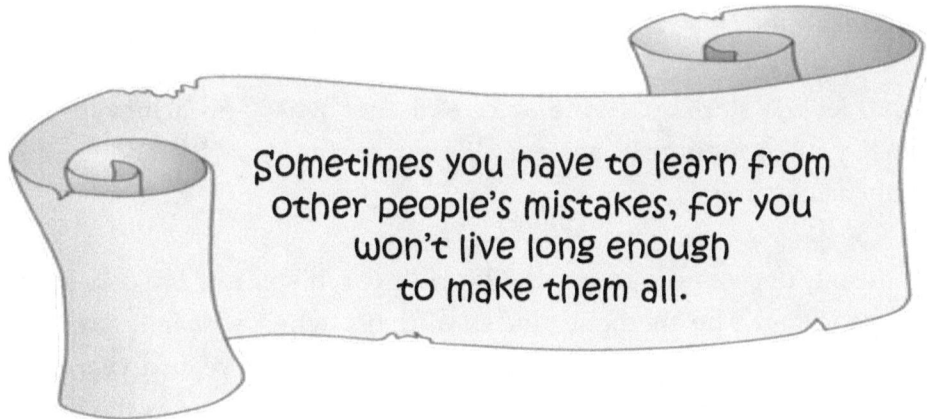

Sometimes you have to learn from other people's mistakes, for you won't live long enough to make them all.

Chapter 6

Abide By the Rules

*G*od works within his principles. Whoever you are, wherever you are, if you abide by HIS principles, all things work for you. It is every person's desire to be successful in life.

As you grew, probably, you pictured yourself driving the car of your dreams, living in that spacious house, and having fat bank accounts that allow you to get whatever you want, whenever you want it. Although at times, we want them for the wrong reasons. The question that still stands is, What is really the key to success? And where is success found?

Well, let me start by saying, success is not what you achieved, but what you continuously achieve. It's not in the past. It's about your daily achievements.

Someone once said success is like riding a bike. You have to keep on paddling. The moment you stop, that's when you fall. Are you excelling, or do you remain the same old person year-in-year-out? Most people do measure success by the number of houses they own or by the type of car they drive.

Now, let us take a look at some of the keys.

We want to come to an understanding of these set principles.

Remember the Lord Your God

S o many times, we tend to lean on our own strength and understanding. Subconsciously, we feel like God does not involve Himself in moneymaking matters, and we tend to put Him on hold until we are done with our own man-devised strategies. That is when we can come before Him to render a tithe and an offering. Wait a minute, God is not interested in our offerings, but our hearts (Ps. 50: 7–15). An offering is in fact for our benefit. We do not pay God with a tithe, but we return.

> *But thou shalt remember the Lord thy God:*
> *for it is He that giveth thee*
> *power to get wealth . . .*
> (Deut. 8: 18, KJV)

There is no better thing than fearing the Lord. It is the grass roots of wisdom. The Bible says, it is the beginning of wisdom. In Job 22, it is said that if we return unto God, we shall be built up. The chapter continues to say that we shall lay up gold like dust, God shall be our defence, and we shall have plenty of silver.

Why is God comparing the abundance of gold with dust, and not stones? Well, the answer is simple. Remember God's promise to Abram, who was named Abraham. He said he will multiply his (*Abraham*) offspring to be as countless as the sand of the seashore. This gives us acuity that God is capable of raising you to a level where you lose count of your own wealth. There are two reasons why God wants to bless men.

> *He will make you rich in every*
> *way so that you can always*
> *give freely. And your giving*
> *Through us will make many to*
> *give thanks to God.*
> (2 Cor. 9: 11, NCV)

God blesses man for him to be a blessing and to bring glory unto His name. In the book of Joel 2: 26, God says that we will have plenty to eat and be full and praise His name.

There is a benefit that comes with fearing the Lord and obeying His commandments.

> *And the Lord shall make thee the*
> *head, and not the tail; and shalt*
> *be above only and thou shalt*
> *not beneath; if that thou hearken*
> *unto the commandments*
> *of the Lord thy God . . .*
> (Deut. 28: 13, KJV)

The Bible also mentions the capability of God to raise a beggar from the dust and make him to sit with the princes.

I was having a talk with a friend of mine, Pastor Ronald, about the rich young ruler, when Jesus told him to sell whatever he has and follow him. The Bible mentions that the young man left sad and sorrowful for he had great possessions. Then Jesus said, 'It's easier for a camel to enter through the eye of a needle than a rich man to enter the kingdom of God.' Jesus didn't mean that rich people are not for the kingdom. This will contradict what He did, when scripture says, 'Though He was rich, for our sake He became poor so that through his poverty we may become rich.'

There are riches that we accumulate outside God's will that makes us feel like it is our own doing. As long as we take the credit, we fail to acknowledge God's sovereignty. That was the situation with the rich young ruler. Those things we got through our own strength are like excess fat that restricts us from entering through the eye of a needle, and by shedding them, we can easily enter, and then accumulate the God-given riches in the kingdom that we do not have to suffer for, and therefore give glory to the Giver. Jesus clearly mentioned in the same text that we shall then have much in this present life and in the life to come. Greatness is certain. We are destined to be blessed.

There are four major lessons I learnt from the life of William Colgate, namely, perseverance, abiding by God's principles, learning, and diversification.

Born in 1783 to a British farmer, William and family moved to New York City due to some political turmoil. His father ventured into some soap-making business with a partner, which didn't work out well. William discovered his interest in the same thing his father failed to set off the ground. He obtained employment as an apprentice soap boiler, where he closely watched and learnt some skills. He also noted mistakes his employer made. That's how his foundation was set up.

He hooked up with dealers from other cities and launched the Colgate Company that we all know.

Intrigued by Genesis 28: 20–22, William made up his mind to abide by biblical principles and give 10 per cent of all his increase. When he realised it works, he personally increased it to 20 per cent. His profits kept on skyrocketing, and he raised it again to 30 per cent.

With time, the company diversified, bringing in more products. Currently, the company is rated one of America's richest.

Give

*a*part from God's word, our ancestors, though they were ignorant of God's principles, realised that a hand that gives always receives, as is proven by their proverbs. These proverbs do appear almost in every language and dialect. This is evidence enough to a non-believing heart that there is something about giving.

In the words of an international speaker and pastor of Bible Life Ministries, talking about money, he says,

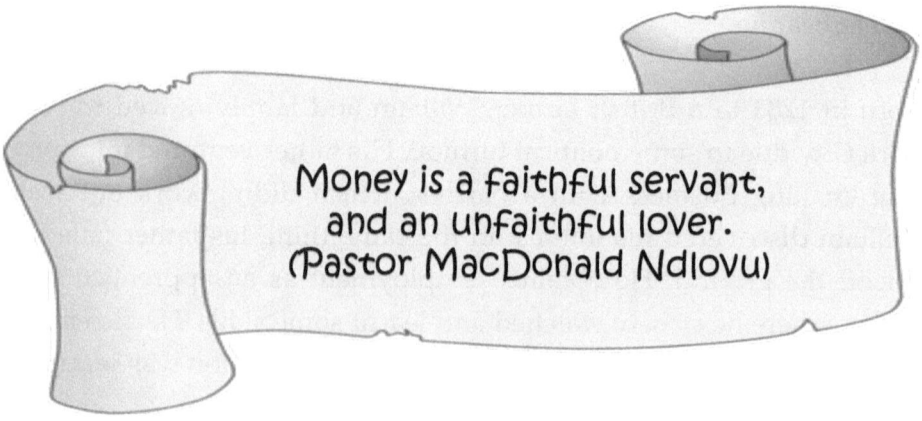

Money is a faithful servant,
and an unfaithful lover.
(Pastor MacDonald Ndlovu)

If you direct much of your love to money so much that you do not want to let it go, the Bible says that you will soon come to lack. Contrary to the world's belief, he who gives liberally shall never lack.

Money should be a servant to you. It should work for you. It is known also as currency because it flows. Money should never be stagnant.

Giving is like sowing a seed in the ground. This is a move of faith, because logically a seed has to die in order for it to produce. This concept has to be understood and acknowledged even more by one who wants to venture into business, because the whole mystery behind sowing is what makes a business. No sowing, no harvesting.

> *Give and it shall be given unto*
> *you; Good measure, pressed*
> *down, shaken together and running*
> *over, shall men give into your bosom.*
> (Luke 6: 38)

Do you notice something about this verse? That, ' . . . It is men, and not angels that shall give back to you.'

It's God who bestows that favour upon you, that will make people want to give or buy from you amongst all others. That is the favour the world seeks after and counterfeits it with charms.

There are two things that determines your harvest, which are the amount of seed and the quality of your soil.

> *Remember this: the person who plants*
> *little will have a small harvest, but the*
> *person who plants a lot will*
> *have a big harvest.*
> (2 Cor. 9: 6, NCV)

This gives us the power to determine our amount of harvest.

As mentioned before, remember that your business is a legal entity. As much as you give individually, so should your business. Even the world system tells you that your business remits tax apart from you. If you want to invoke God's blessing over your business, consider it as an entity. Allow it to tithe.

1. First Fruits

First fruits are simply one's first profits or harvest from his undertaking. This could be when one begins work or business. It can as well be annual. In other words, you will be acknowledging the enabling of God in what you are doing. You will also be sanctifying what follows after.

> *Honor the Lord with your wealth*
> *and the firstfruits from all your crops.*
> *Then your barns will be full, and*
> *Your wine barrels will overflow*
> *with new wine.*
> (Prov. 3: 9–10, NCV)

People are less informed of first fruits than they are of tithes and offerings. God is the one who gives the ability to make wealth. *(Deut. 26: 1–2).* We show that acknowledgement by bringing unto God the first fruits.

2. Tithes and Offerings

Tithe

Tithe is a tenth of your income, which is not necessarily in the form of cash, as many believe. Cash ended up being used often because of the age we are living in. Money has become the main and more compactable medium of exchange.

> *Bring to the storehouse a full tenth*
> *of what you earn so there will be*
> *food in my house.*
> (Mal. 3: 10, NCV)

We do not pay tithe, for we cannot pay God. Can we afford to pay for all He has done for us? We return, that's why the word of God says 'bring'. He entrusts us with everything; then He says bring what is mine. God allows us to receive all, and then He says, 'remove and bring back what is mine.' Tithe in my own words is a test of faithfulness. Him who can't be trusted with little, can't be trusted with much.

Tithe brings security. That's why God says, He will rebuke the devourer. Accidents and losses are covered.

There are certain situation we go through simply because there is no covering over our possessions.

Offering

An offering is out of free will. This is where most of us fail, because offering is when we show how much we trust God with our possessions. That's an opportunity to show how much we love Him. This means that an offering should be more than a tithe. A tithe is simply 10 per cent, but an offering can be more than that.

Your offering speaks for you. Your offering is like a point of contact. In the old days, people wouldn't go before God or a prophet of God empty-handed. That's why Saul, the time he was desperately looking for his father's donkeys, said, ' . . . we can't go before the man of God empty-handed.' At times, I wonder why it becomes so difficult for our community to understand this concept, looking at the fact that before we knew Christ, we couldn't dare go before those traditional doctors and fortune-tellers empty-handed. It seems we understood the notion of a seed. Now that we are where it originates, how do we afford to miss it?

The Power of Confession

In the beginning, God created the heaven and earth. Interestingly, He spoke a word and things came into existence. He continues to say, *'let us make man in our own image . . .'* Nature tells us that every living thing produces according to its kind. Meaning, if God created man after His kind, then there is a godly gene in man. If God has the power of creation on His lips, it simply means that if man reiterates God's declarations over his life, those things will definitely come to pass.

That authority was vested in us.

Then the Lord reached out
His hand and touched my mouth. (v9)
. . . you will pull up and tear down,
destroy and overthrow,
build up and plant. (v10)
(Jer. 1: 9–10)

The main purpose of words is to create. This makes me wonder why God had to make Zechariah unable to speak until after the child's birth. It could probably be, because God didn't want him to say anything negative anymore, like he did when the angel Gabriel came to deliver the message. His lips were only loosened when he was naming the child according to God's command.

I remember talking to a friend of mine Obert saying, 'Have you ever observed something about witches? They don't need to go into the bush, hunting for some *weed or roots* to bewitch someone. All they need is an altar and a word. They curse with their mouths.' The enemy is good at counterfeiting God's ideas. Remember Pharaoh's magicians (Exod. 7: 8–12). They counterfeited snakes as well. However, Aaron's swallowed them all. Thank God that we are made victors in Jesus name.

There are people whose names God had to change in order for them to fit in His great plan. People like Abram (exalted father). God had to name him Abraham *(father of many nations)* because that is where God was taking him. Here is the secret: each time people and God himself called him Abraham, it was a confession. When he answers, it was like an agreement, just as one saying, 'Yes, I am, the father of many nations.' The same happened with Jacob (Israel), Simon (Peter), and Saul (Paul).

Confession goes hand-in-hand with faith. You confess and act according to what you are believing in your heart.

We create things in the spiritual. This makes things to become factual and tangible in the spiritual realm first, then later manifest in the physical. The physical will be like a replay of the spiritual. Watch this:

> *Faith is the substance of things*
> *hoped for, and the evidence*
> *of things not seen.*
> (Heb. 11: 1, KJV)

Some manuscripts like NCV says, ' . . . and knowing that something is real even if we do not see it.' In the book of Revelations, John saw things to come. As he states it, it's in past tense as the battle has already been won. That is where confession comes in. What you speak is what you become. You can speak your way to your breakthrough and the other way round.

> *No weapon that is formed against thee*
> *shall prosper; and every tongue that shall rise*
> *up against thee in judgment*
> *thou shalt condemn . . .*
> (Isa. 54: 17, KJV)

There is an interesting part in this verse that says, ' . . . and *every tongue that shall rise up against you in judgment* thou shalt condemn'. Take note of something here; it is not for God to condemn but *you*. Make it your daily routine to make declarations of who you want to become. Even if it takes time, speak it.

Jesus cursed the fig tree and he went away. There was no any immediate sign of response, until the following morning (*Mark 11:*

12–15). He continued with journey as planned. The disciples got the shock of their lives. Whilst passing again, they found the fig tree having withered.

> *The next morning as Jesus*
> *was passing by with his followers,*
> *they saw the tree dry and*
> *dead, even to the roots.*
> (Mark 11: 20, NCV)

God's word once spoken, it sticks, despite the time taken. Do not worry when you speak and it seems like it's adding up to nothing.

Kings and Priests

The word of God tells us that we are *kings* and *priests*.

It is the duty of a king to decree:

> *Thou shalt also decree a thing,*
> *and it shall be established unto thee:*
> (Job 22: 28, KJV)

To understand this concept, you need to have an idea of a monarchy and a republic.

Republic

A president leads a republic, backed by a cabinet and governed by a constitution. A republic has democracy. This means that the people have a say in the drafting of a constitution, which is done through voting. A president is elected in and out of power, and his powers are limited. A republic has parliamentarians who are elected by the people, meaning that they can be from a different political background, having different views.

Kingdom

This seems to be the opposite of a republic. A kingdom consists of a king and a domain. A domain is a sphere of influence. In a monarchy notion of leadership, a king is not designated, but automatically comes into power because of blood lineage. His royal subjects pay homage to him. Whatever a king decrees goes. His word is final, and his only source of influence are his advisors.

> *Now, oh king, establish the*
> *decree, and sign the writing*
> *that it not be changed ,...*
> (Dan. 6: 8, KJV)

Now, when the word of God tells us that we are kings, it means we have that power to declare things uncontested. That's the kingdom, and there is no democracy about that. Remember this applies both in the positive and in the negative.

This also means that we should be careful of what we say. Never speak carelessly, for it has an effect be it in the positive or negative. That's why the word says, we shall be held accountable of every word that we speak.

> *Then the officer who was close*
> *to the king answered Elisha,*
> *'Even if the Lord opened windows*

in the sky, that couldn't happen.'
Elisha said, 'You will see
it with your eyes, but you
will not eat any of it.'
(2 Kgs. 7: 2, NCV)

At times people disqualify themselves from God's blessing by simply speaking. You can confess in line with God's word and succeed, or speak against it and disqualify yourself.

Priests

The priest, according to the Bible, stands in the presence of God to offer sacrifices and supplications as well as make atonement *(Lev. 15: 14–15)*. This wasn't meant to be for everyone, but thanks be to God who qualified us through the blood of Jesus. Only priests can boldly stand in His presence.

Thou shalt make thy prayer to Him
and He shall hear thee . . .
(Job 22: 27, KJV)

If you go through both the verses 27 and 28 of Job 22, you realise that the service of a priest comes first. What it means is, make your requests known to God in prayer. Never shun prayer, for it is the conduit that connects you to your power source. Imagine an electrical gadget sitting next to a power source, but without a power cable. That's how we can be without prayer. Scripture says, 'Pray without ceasing.' Jesus gave a parable of a power widow who continually came before the shrewd judge, asking for vindication over her adversaries. At times, we come before God with options. We do pray with hope in a friend or relative, in case if prayer doesn't yield our anticipated results. One preacher once said, one wouldn't mind to spend a night in a long queue just to acquire a visa to travel to wherever he wants to go, than being patient in God's presence for an answer.

Never pray positively and declare negatively. It's better to remain silent than to nullify what you would have built in the spirit realm.

There is yet an interesting part of this verse. The second part of verse 27 says, . . . *and thou shalt pay thy vows.* It's better to owe man than God. Always make sure you pay your dues to God. That's your other secret to success.

At times, you simply need a man of God to speak a word over your life. All it took Hannah was just a simple word from a man of God to bring a miracle she couldn't get in years.

We are kings and priests. What a great privilege and honour it is!

Winners are fighters who do not quit.

Your Title Deed

*W*hen one owns a piece of land, the guarantee that he has of land ownership is his possession of the title deed. This indicates the details, size, and address of the land. This serves also as proof that the state recognises your ownership. In this case, one can live without fear of eviction at any given time. The word of God is your title deed. He says,

'For I watch over my word to perform it.'
(Jer. 1: 12, KJV)

So shall my word be that goeth
forth out of my mouth: it shall not
return unto me void, but it shall
accomplish that which I please, and
it shall prosper in the thin
whereto I sent it
(Isa. 55: 11, KJV)

This verse contains two interesting keywords. These are *accomplish* and *prosper*. Accomplishing is achieving or completing. This means that God makes sure that whatever He spoke is done to completion. To prosper is to flourish or to show profit. Whatever God says concerning you has to be completed as well as accompanied by burgeoning results. Many of us may not have a problem with reading the word, but putting it into action. The word of God is not like a story that you read and all it does is make you feel good. Its more than that. It is living and active. Meaning it has power to activate your situation. Peter understood this better, that all he needed was the word.

Peter said, 'Lord, if it is really
you, then command me to

come to you on the water.'
Jesus said, 'Come.'
(Matt. 14: 28–29, NCV).

Only at Jesus's word did Peter do an extraordinary thing of walking on water.

Get to know what the word says, and stand on whatever He said in His word concerning your life. Make it your ground. Do not put your focus on circumstances around you. Just take God's living word as it is, and believe it. Many are things God promised to those who love Him.

Chapter 7

Get Out of Debt

a borrower is always a slave to the lender. In the world we are living nowadays, due to the introduction of credit cards and other credit facilities, the majority of people are living in abject debt. A thing that was once an embarrassment in the yesteryears now has become tolerable. For the sake of luring clients to themselves, some even offer down to 0 per cent deposit, though they know that once you possess their merchandise, you have fallen into their dungeon. Many people are paying through the nose, having become slaves to debt.

Getting yourself into an unnecessary debt is like reaping into the future to suffice the present need. Nevertheless, the fact is, when you reach into the future, you are going to meet yet another deficiency. You may as well end up needing a debt to pay a debt.

And thou shalt lend unto many
nations, and thou shalt not borrow
(Deut. 28: 12b, KJV)

Have you at some point ever thought of it this way that it is on God's top desires that we live totally a debt-free life? It is true.

If you are not in debt, maintain it that way. The secret lies behind living within your means and not a pace set by people around you.

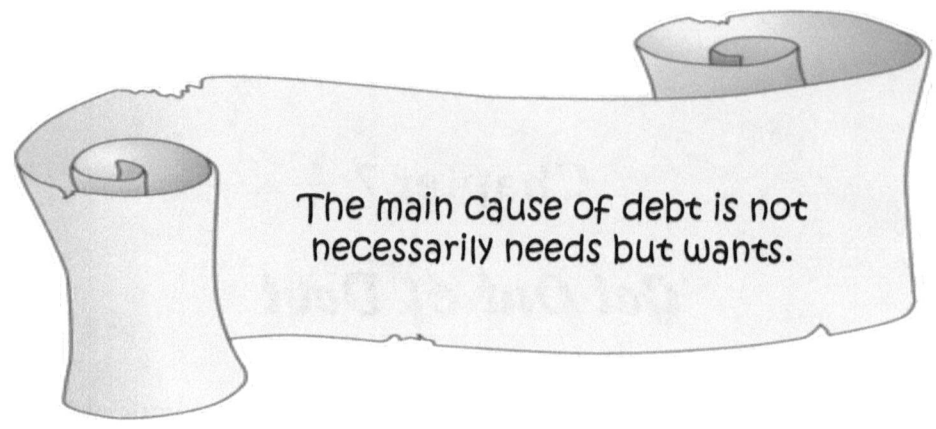

The main cause of debt is not necessarily needs but wants.

Saving Saves

Have you ever realised that a person who earns as little as $300 a month and one earning $3,000, both complain, but still survive. Both may opt for a debt to supplement their income, though they can still survive without. Now the question is, if one earning less can survive within his means, why then can't the latter endure a little suffering to obtain a better future, than enjoying for a while and suffer for long? This proves that it is not about how much one brings home, but how those funds are managed. Many are ignorant of financial management and saving in particular. If I may wander a bit. Let us take a look at some of the silly mistakes we make.

For instance, an item bought on lay-by is most likely to be more than twice cheaper than that bought on hire purchase, though it feels as if you will be paying lesser monthly instalments. However, how many people are patient enough to wait, save, and buy either on cash or on lay-by?

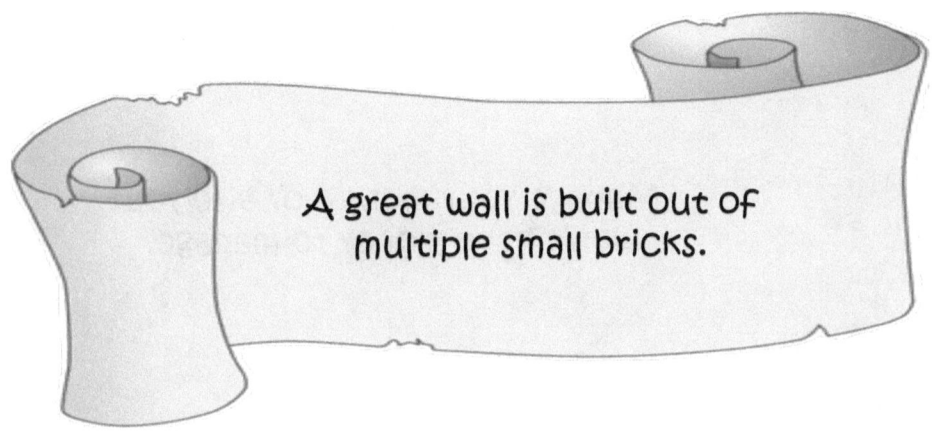

A great wall is built out of multiple small bricks.

Learn to save from the little you have. Our God is not a wasteful God. After feeding the five thousand men (John 6: 12), the leftovers were gathered, filling twelve baskets. Jesus didn't say, 'Ooh, now that you had enough, you can dispose the remainder into the lake.' Instead, he said, 'Gather the leftovers so that nothing is wasted.'

In a lifetime, it's not about how much you made, but how much you saved. We've seen and heard of businesspeople, sportsman, and musicians, who became millionaires, but ended their career in debt.

Haven't you heard of people who won lotto and became instant millionaires overnight, but died a pauper? This is a common thing year in year out. Now, the question is, what could be the problem? Well, the secret lies in saving and good financial management.

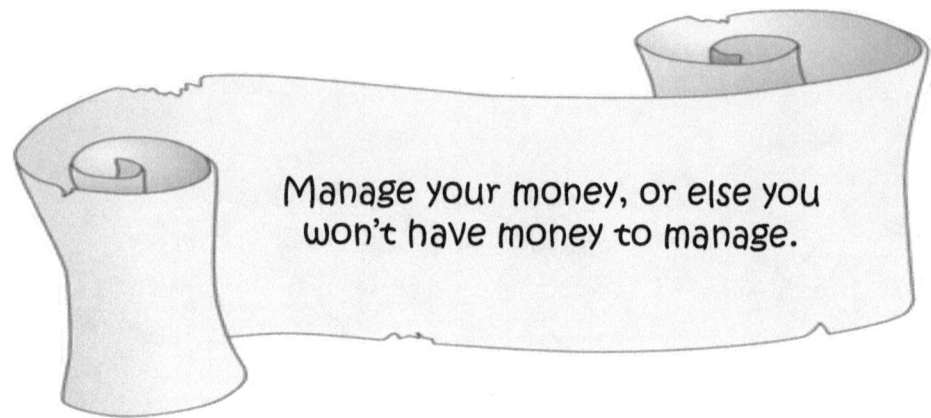

Manage your money, or else you won't have money to manage.

Employ the pen and paper magic. A human is a supercomputer with a less-effective memory. We tend to forget so quickly. That is why writing things down helps. Set for yourself financial goals. Write them down. State when you want to reach them, and what you must do to realise them.

Learn to live within your means. At all costs, fight to spend less than what you earn and invest the rest.

Most people are *dollar wise and cent foolish*. We seem to be more conscious when it comes to larger amounts of money than smaller amounts.

That is why it is easy for many to cast coins and smaller notes on the altar in churches. It is unconsciously a way of disposing the unwanted, as much as we do into a beggar's purse. If one has coins in his pockets, he or she tends to buy things that are not necessary needs or on the budget, as a way of clearing pockets. Little do we realise that a dollar is made up of multiple cents. You can agree with me that many of us when we have a currency note, we fear breaking it, because once the change comes in smaller notes and coins, we tend to abuse it and fail to account for it. Be disciplined and save.

You can open a savings account. Name it whatever you like. In this account, you deposit any small amounts you think are too small to achieve a thing. Like what I chose to do, you can as well open an account that you have less access to, and arrange for a stop order of at least 10 per cent of your monthly income and have it transferred into that savings account. Learn to save whilst you are doing well, so that when harsh times knock on your door, you will be able to keep your head above the water. Economies are bound to change.

Assets versus Liabilities

Wisdom is the answer to our problems, not money. There are monetary riches, and there is wealth *(accumulated in the form of possessions)*. One can become monetary rich anytime and lose it just as quick as he got it. Whereas the other can accumulate wealth over a space of time that will last for generations.

The African community for years have been moving in the same vicious cycle. The first thirty years of life are spend trying to amend financial errors made by parents. One has to provide for the parents and siblings. The other twenty years are shared between bringing up their own family and trying to build their own lives. Before they know it, they would have gone past retirement age. This would mean their kids have to follow the same track, and there is no room to save for an inheritance. The scripture says, *'a good man leaves an inheritance for his children. Even for his children's children.'*

Robert T Kiyosaki, the author of *Rich dad, poor dad,* mentioned one imperative thing the upper class understand, which the poor and middle class don't.

The rich invests in assets, whereas the poor and middle class invest in liabilities. There are liabilities that we cannot live without. The point is, invest more in assets than in liabilities. Our major challenge mostly is we are not ready to endure for a little while.

Let's try to come to an understanding of assets and liabilities in a simplified way.

Liabilities

Liabilities are those things that mostly depreciate in value, and they do not bring income. They actually survive on your pocket. They are like a parasite. For instance, if one decides to buy for himself a luxurious 4.2-litre engine car that requires special service, and it does not generate cash, but rather milk his pockets, it means he owns a liability.

By the way, did you know that a car starts wearing out the moment you start the engine? In other words, it starts losing value the moment you start its engine. We can't live totally without liabilities. Some liabilities are as well essential in our daily lives. For example, a car is essential for convenience in moving.

Life is in stages. You have to pass through all of them until you reach the top. There is a stage where you can afford a car as a necessity. This is determined by your capacity to maintain it without strain. Before you buy that car, the question you need to ask yourself is 'With my current financial status, is it necessary to own one?' If you realise that it's necessary to own one, which one can you afford to maintain without having to struggle to keep your head above the water? There is a level where a car moves from being a necessity to being a luxury. This isn't a level you reach overnight. It comes with hard work. It is determined by your financial stability. Your liabilities should never surpass your assets.

Assets

Assets are actually the opposite of liabilities. They fall into two categories. That is *fixed assets* and *current assets* also known as circulating assets. Fixed assets are long-term durable properties, whereas current assets are those goods that can easily be converted to cash.

Assets do appreciate in value, and they do generate income. For example, if one owns a house, when inflation hits, it actually appreciates in price or rentals, if you choose to let. One is more secure owning assets than liabilities.

Mostly, we do things for acceptance in society. However, the question is, does the society really care?

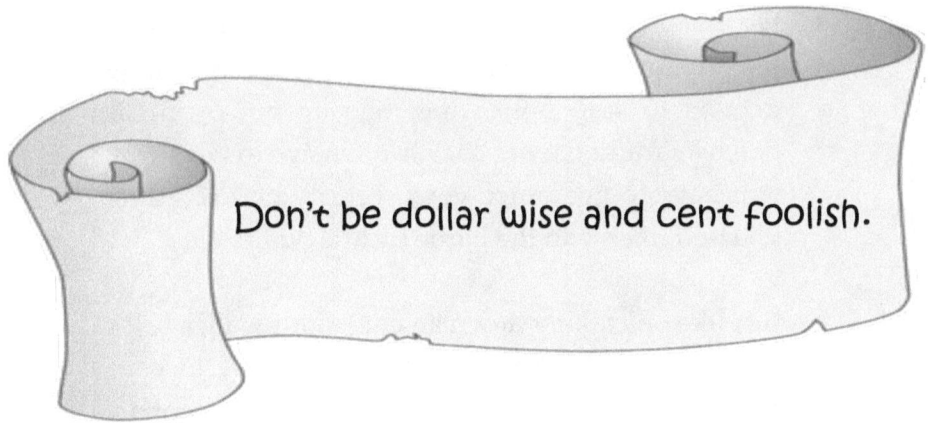

Don't be dollar wise and cent foolish.

My Dirty Debt

Are you in debt? *Gosh!* It doesn't feel good! Debt, like a drug, is addictive. Once you start it, you keep on telling yourself that you can and you will pay up. Little do you realise that the reason for your incessant borrowing is a sign of you're not having the capacity to take care of those needs or wants financially. Before you realise it, you are in a huge debt. However, thank goodness, it's never too late.

Of course, debt is not a thing you can just close your eyes to and 'Swoosh', it disappears. That is only read in fairy tales. You have to face and conquer your giants, despite what it takes. Sometimes debt is like a scary gigantic wall standing right in front of us. What stresses us the most is how to make it disappear in a split of a second, so that we can be free again. At times even wishing you could wake up the lucky person, having won the lotto prize and pompously stand in front of your creditor and ask him to name his price. This can just be a fantasy.

This is how you go about it.

- Debt is a malady, but thank goodness, there is an remedy for it. The first and foremost step to treating debt is to stop borrowing. Seizing borrowing is defensive, and paying back is offensive. As in a war, you have to guarantee your security by defending yourself, then win the battle by attacking.

- Just like one taking down an enormous wall, a brick at a time, that is how you find your way to your freedom. If it's a moderate debt, try to negotiate with your creditor on how much you can afford to pay in instalments, and agree on the period, even if it attracts an extra interest. If you are dealing with multiple small debts, you need to consider a consolidating loan. This is one major loan that pays up all your small loans or debts, leaving you managing one. This allows you to pay back flexibly over a period of time with a manageable interest rate.

- Be financially disciplined. Learn to draft a budget. Sometimes we overlook the importance of budgeting. A budget is like a map that shows where you are going and how you will get there. If you draft one, stick to it. Do not waver from your budget, even if what you see seems to be too good to resist. Do not buy what isn't necessarily a crucial need.

- Try spreading your needs over a period of time, giving priorities. This goes without saying, honour your instalments. Do not tell yourself that you can always double up the payment on the next instalment. This has two major effects. The first one being that it can cost you trust from your creditor. Secondly, you may never know what the other month holds.

- You need to make a sacrifice. Let go from your budget certain things that you can do without. It allows you to have a surplus from your tight budget. This can help you in paying up your dues.

- If you realise that you are an addict to debt, seek help. Do not deceive yourself saying you can conquer your wars alone. You might need counselling. Revealing your problem to a trustworthy person is a step towards your healing. A thing that you can openly confess to someone, you cannot easily fall into the same trap again.

Salvation

I believe this manuscript has been of great help to you. However, for you to fully enjoy these benefits, you need to have a relationship with the God of the benefits. The Bible says, *'but to all who did accept Him and believe in Him He gave the right to become children of God.'* (John 1: 12)

If you have never had such an opportunity, why don't you invite Him in your life now?

Say this prayer from the bottom of your heart:

Lord Jesus, I acknowledge that I am a sinner.

Forgive me of my sins.

Come into my heart, and make me a new creature.

Thank you for making me a child of God. I declare that I am born-again: I am a child of God, in Jesus's name.

Amen

Appendix

Confession—speaking of a thing either negatively or positively, which therefore has power to influence its outcome.

First fruits—what one gets as his first harvest. It could be in the form of cash or produce.

Impulsive Buying—buying more than necessary.

Realm—a sphere of influence.

Au fait—in control of a thing.

Haggle—a bargain.

Opportunist—an investor.

The Blue Ocean Strategy—a business strategy whereby one focuses on improving the quality of his products to lure the market.

Personal Touch—having a one-on-one relationship with clients.

Legal Entity—an officially recognised unit or body.

Hoodwink—to deceive.

Captivating—being attractive or charming.

Diligence—being hardworking or industrious.

Tithe—a tenth of your total income.

Notes

Notes

Notes

Notes

Notes

Index